MY AXOLOTL LIFE

by FB Smit
illustrated by Brooke O'Neill

PICTURE WINDOW BOOKS
a capstone imprint

Published by Picture Window Books,
an imprint of Capstone
1710 Roe Crest Drive
North Mankato, Minnesota 56003
capstonepub.com

Library of Congress Cataloging-in-Publication Data is available on the Library of Congress website.
ISBN: 9798875239250 (hardcover)
ISBN: 9798875239205 (paperback)
ISBN: 9798875239212 (ebook PDF)

Summary: Discover what a day in the life of a Wild Type axolotl would be like, from what it eats to how it stays safe.

Editorial Credits
Editor: Christianne Jones
Designer: Kay Fraser
Production Specialist: Whitney Schaefer

Printed and bound in China. PO 6461

Hi! I'm Axolotl—a Wild Type axolotl to be exact. See how my brown body blends in with my **environment**?

Can you guess how that helps me?

Because it keeps me safe! I’m always on the alert for predators. Once, a carp and tilapia chased me at the same time!

Guess what I did to escape?

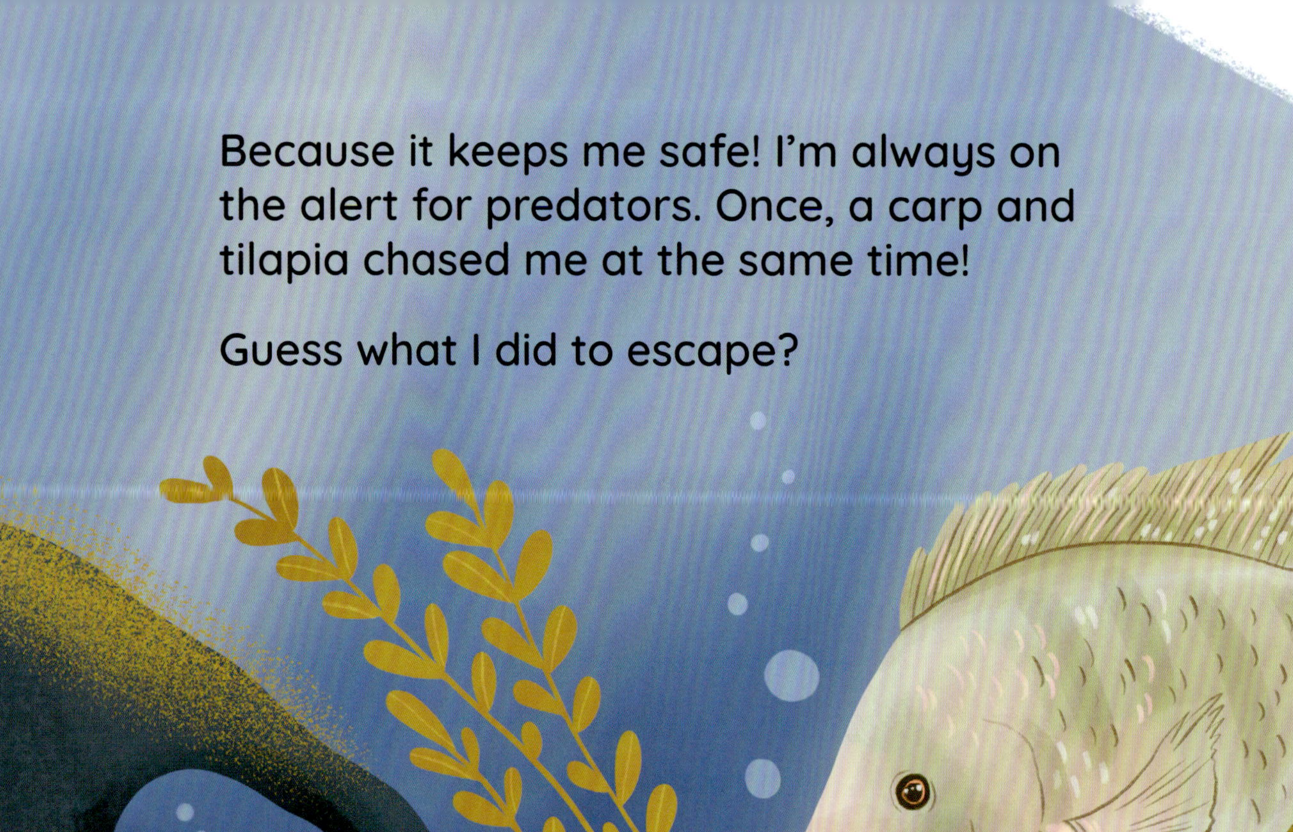

Do you think I hid behind a big plant?

Or did I dig a hole in the lake bottom?

BOTH! I dug a hole and hid behind a plant! I'm smart like that.

Even so, a carp chomped my back, chewed my gills, and gashed my eyeball!

So how come I'm still alive?

Because my parts grew back! That's called regeneration. You can see why scientists study axolotls.

On land or in water, no fish or animal can replace parts exactly the way I can.

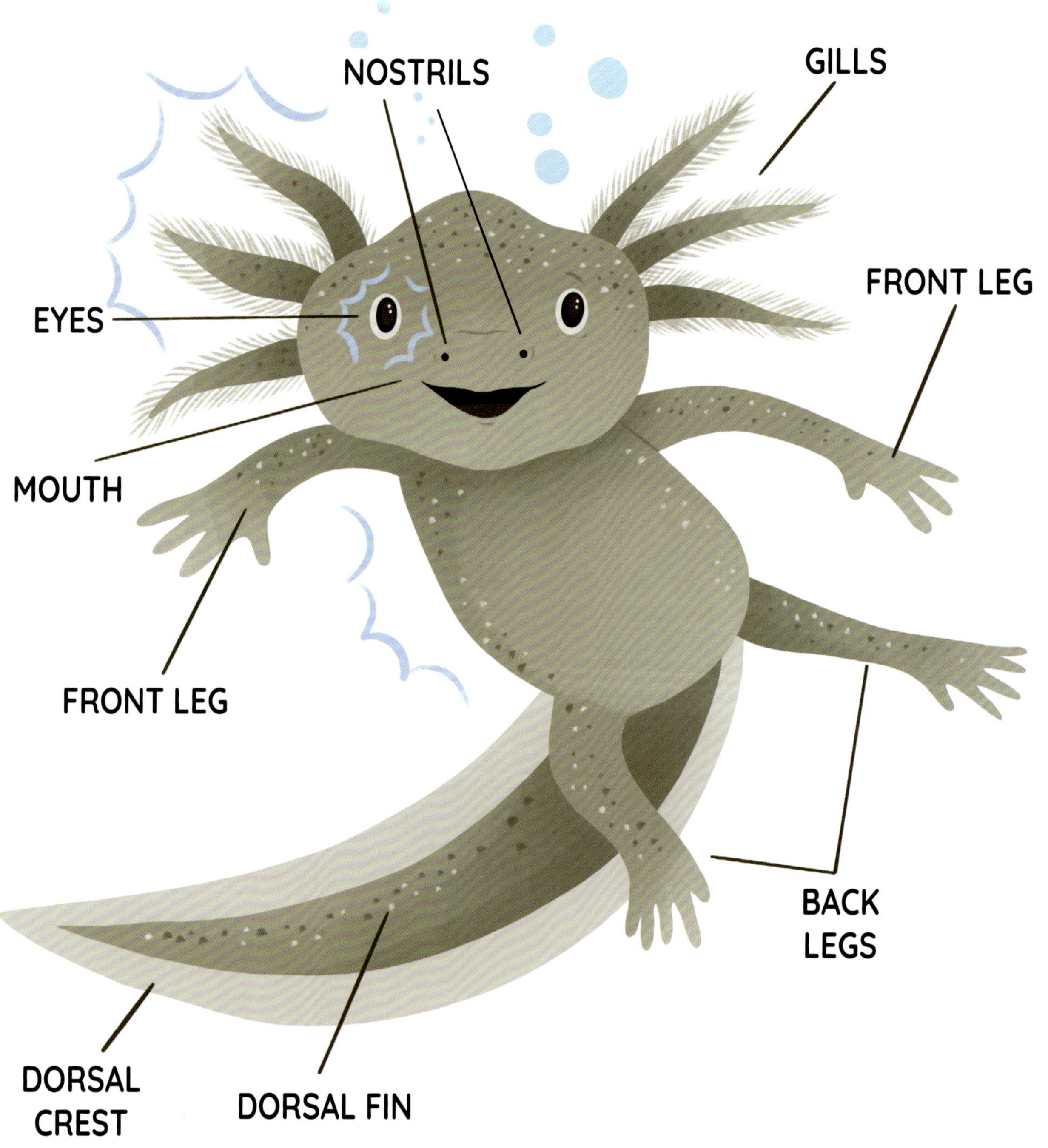

Let me take you back to the beginning.

My grandparents lived in Lake Xochimilco in Mexico. You say that "Zok-i-mil-ko" by the way. There were a lot of us living in that lake.

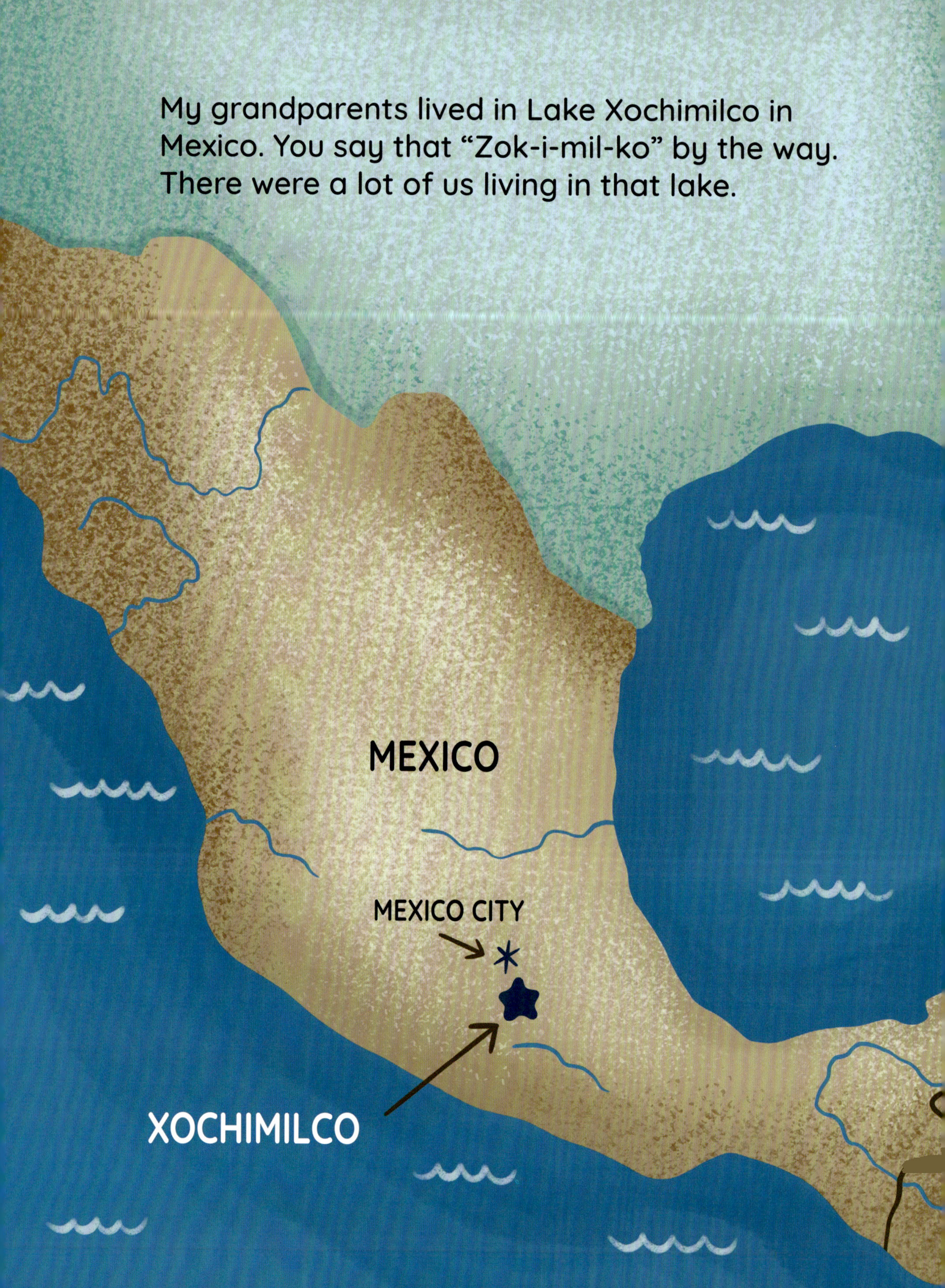

But our home shrank. The lake got dirty. Fish ate my family. Now, there are fewer than 100 axolotls living in our native lake.

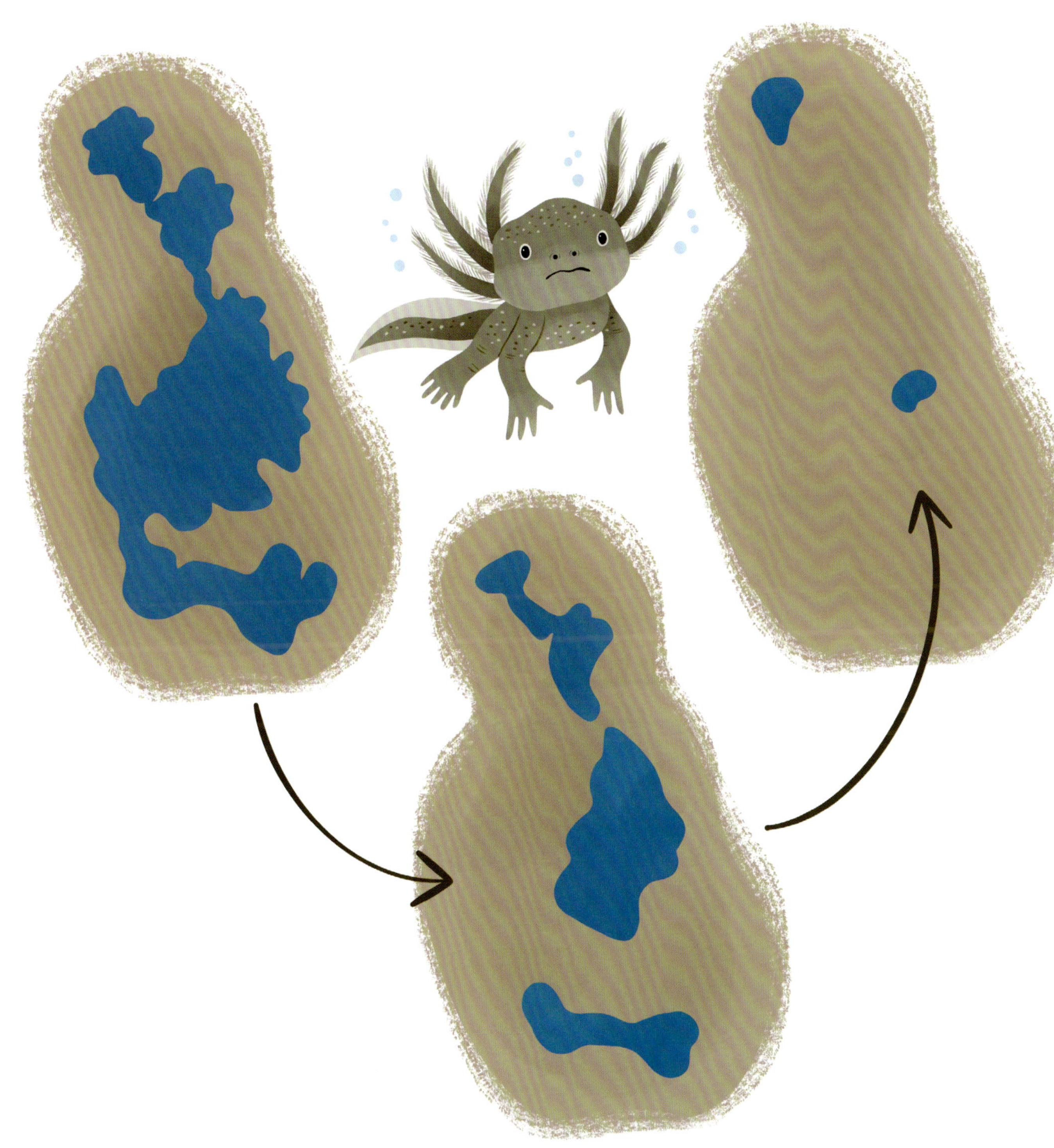

I have loads of cousins. They're not from the wild, but their colors sure are!

They don't need camouflage because they were born for pet life and for scientific studies. They are studied to help prevent our extinction.

Lake Xochimilco's cool, slow-moving, fresh water made the best home. It was not too bright and had a lot of places to hide.

Why do I like to hide?

Because of sunlight—and eyelids. The sun is bright, and I don't have eyelids to block it.

I have other tricks to protect me from the sun, like burrowing in mud and vegetation.

When I'm not hiding, I might be hunting.

Can you guess when I hunt?

At night! I hope you guessed this since I gave you plenty of clues. While I don't have night vision, I DO have smell vision.

I walk-swim along the muddy water bottom, following my superpower nose. I sniff out fish, worms, insects, and shrimp, slurping them up with my strong-as-a-vacuum suction powers.

Know what else? Most amphibians live in water AND on land. Not me.

Thanks to my super-duper gills, I'm all water all the time.

They aren't moving just to say hi. They're getting oxygen from the water. The faster my gills move, the more oxygen I breathe. They wave faster when I'm scared too.

Most amphibians change and lose their cute as they age. Just check out that frog!

But we axolotls keep our cute, baby-fish look as we age. It's called neoteny. The same adorable me from day one. What you see is what you get.

I'm soft and squishy and so very cute, but please don't touch me. I have very sensitive skin. I appreciate an admiring glance, but I like my space.

Speaking of space, any thoughts
on my living arrangements?

If you guessed that I prefer to live alone, you get me. This is awkward for me to tell you, but axolotls eat other axolotls.

No wonder we are loners! We prefer space and places to hide.

So where do I live now?

In a floating garden! This garden's protected water is like living in the wild but with less danger.

I hope there will be more of us one day so we are no longer critically endangered. Because, as you've learned, we are amazing amphibians.

Thanks for spending the day with me!

Awesome Axolotl Facts

- Axolotl means “strange water monster” in Nahuatl, an Uto-Aztecan language spoken in Mexico.
- Axolotls are a type of salamander.
- Instead of sleeping for long periods of time, axolotls go through short sleep cycles throughout the day and night.
- Axolotls come in lots of colors and patterns, including speckled, pink, gold, lavender, and striped.
- Female axolotls can lay up to 1,000 eggs at a time. It takes about two to three weeks for an egg to hatch.
- Axolotls aren’t picky eaters. They eat everything from worms and fish to insects and crustaceans.
- Axolotls do not have teeth. They eat using suction power.

Glossary

amphibian (am-FIB-ee-uhn)—an animal that lives on land and in water

camouflage (KAM-uh-flahzh)—covering that makes animals, people, and objects look like their surroundings

critically endangered (KRIT-ik-lee en-DAYN-jerd)—extremely high risk of disappearing in the wild

environment (en-VAHY-ruhn-muhnt)—the air, water, trees, and other natural surroundings

extinction (ik-STINGK-shuhn)—complete disappearance

gills (GILZ)—a body part on the side of a fish that is used to breathe

native (NAY-tiv)—growing or living naturally in a particular place

neoteny (nee-OT-n-ee)—retaining child-like characteristics into adulthood

oxygen (OK-suh-juhn)—a colorless gas in the air that people and animals need to breathe

predator (PRED-uh-tor)—an animal that hunts other animals for food

regeneration (ri-jen-uh-RAY-shuhn)—regrow a body part

About the Author

FB Smit is an author, blogger, and a preschool teacher. When she's not engaging with the littles at school, she's incubating her real and made-up stories. She's grateful for her husband and children who teach her about life and who thicken her stories' plots. At home near Atlanta, Georgia, FB does her best to avoid buying more houseplants and drinking way too much tea. Connect with her at fbsmit.com.

About the Illustrator

Brooke O'Neill is an illustrator and graphic designer who has illustrated greeting cards, stickers, and more than twenty children's books. When she's not drawing, Brooke loves spending time with her kids, husband, and pets in the suburbs of Chicago. Other interests include playing the ukulele, reading, insects, astrology, sharks, plants, and watching movies. If she wasn't an artist, she would definitely be a professional organizer!